I0463939

LOW LIFE SERIES

Amusing Swear Words To Color

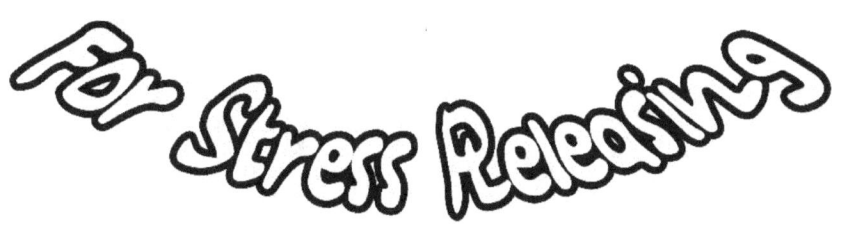

For Stress Releasing

By

Queenie McJody

Copyright © 2017 by Queenie McJody

All rights reserved worldwide. No part of this publication may be reproduced or distributed in any form or by any means, mechanical, electronic or stored in a retrieval or database system, without written permission from the copyright holder.

Happy Coloring!

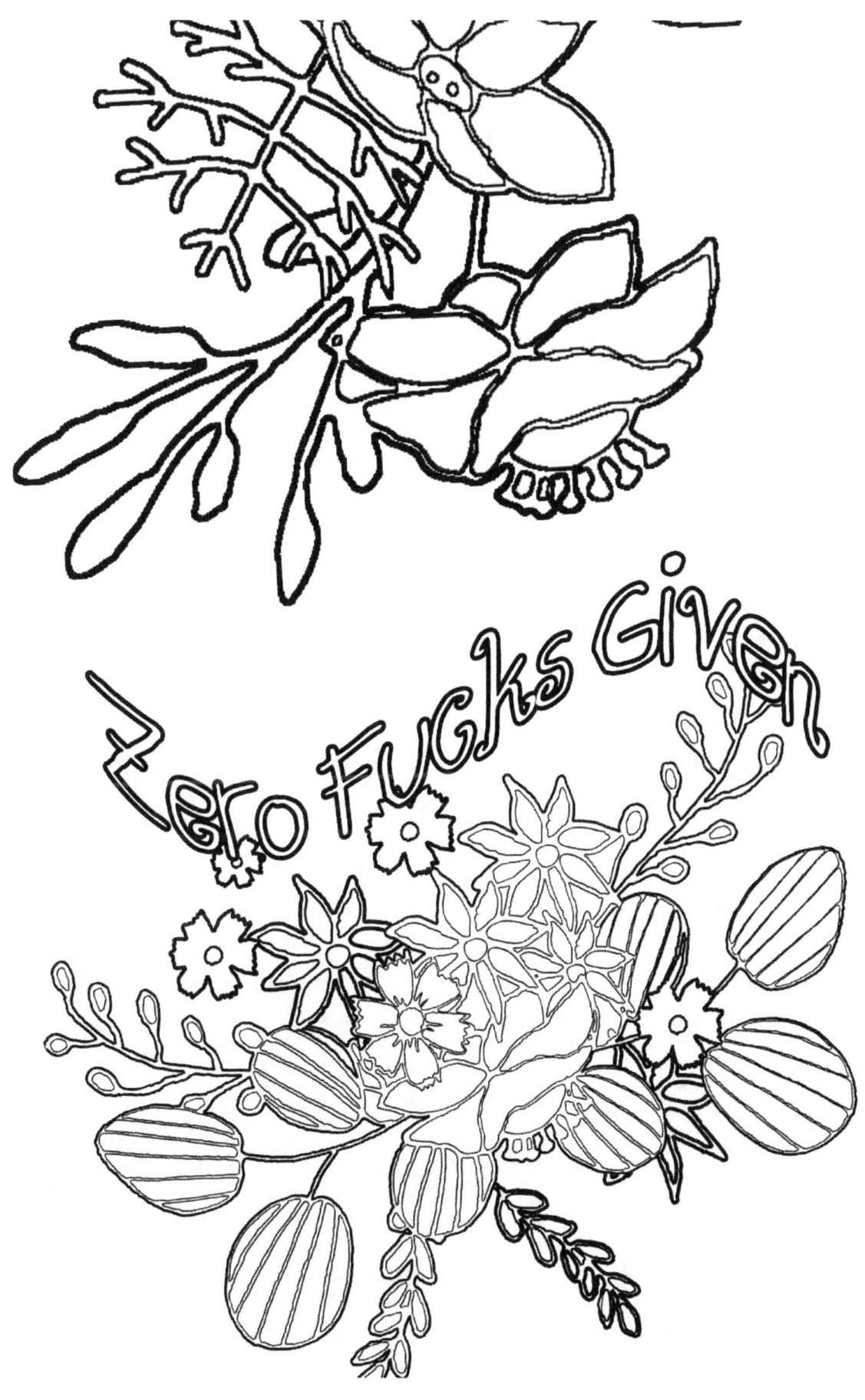

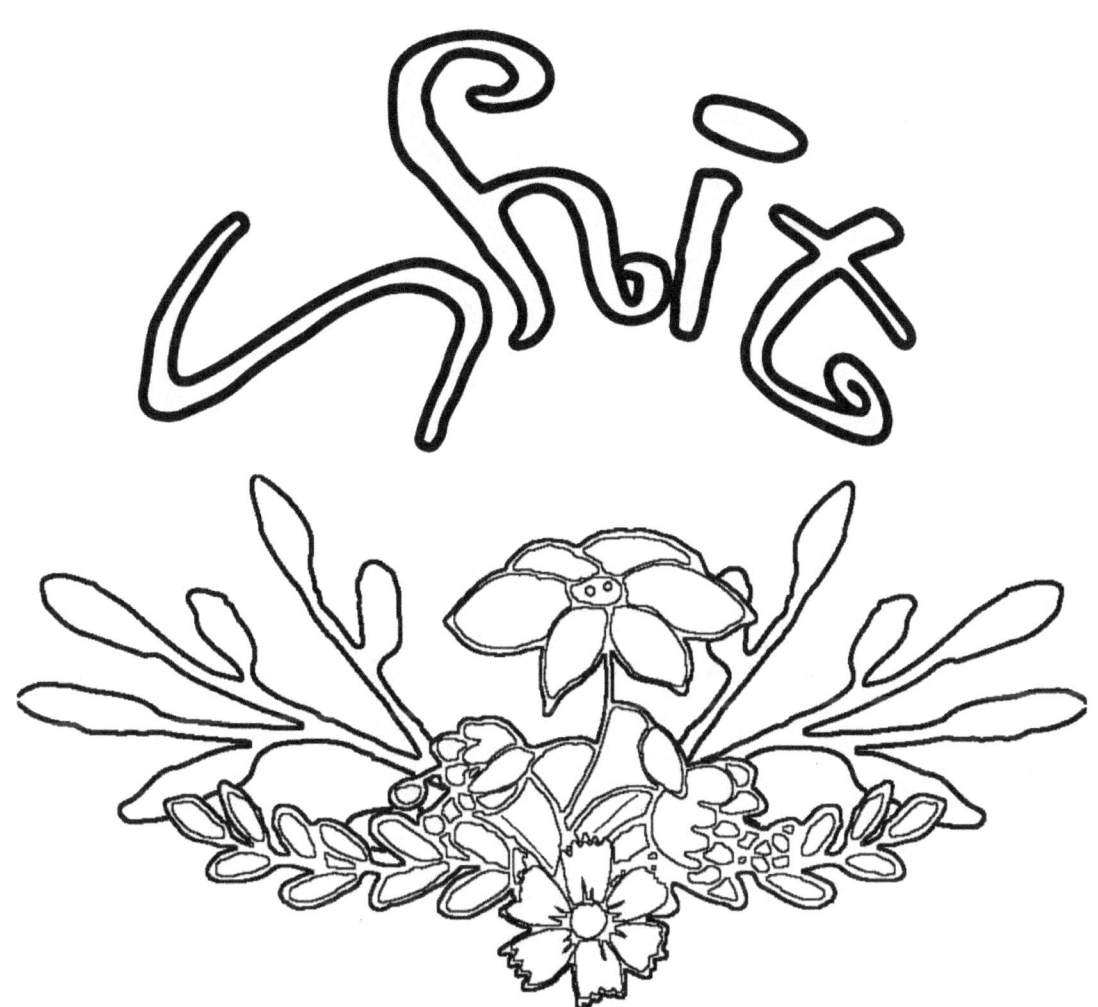

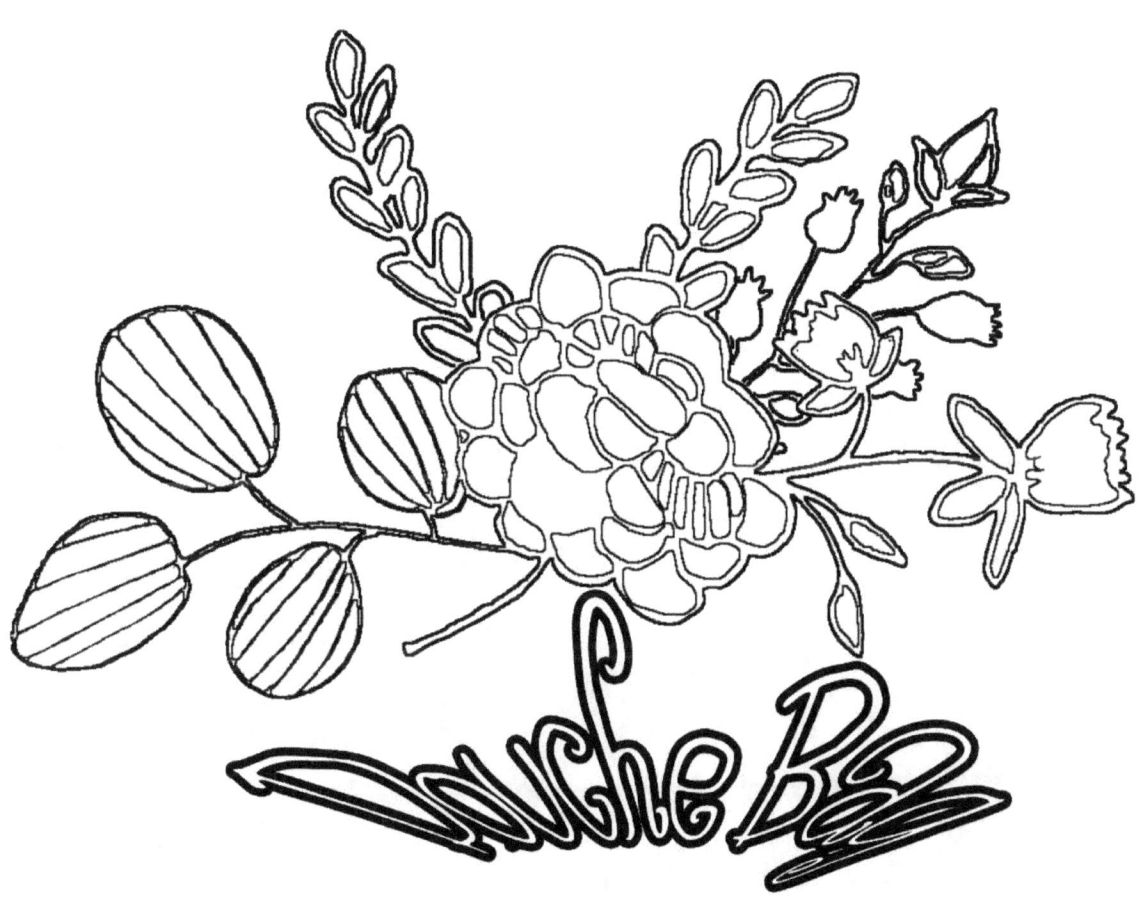

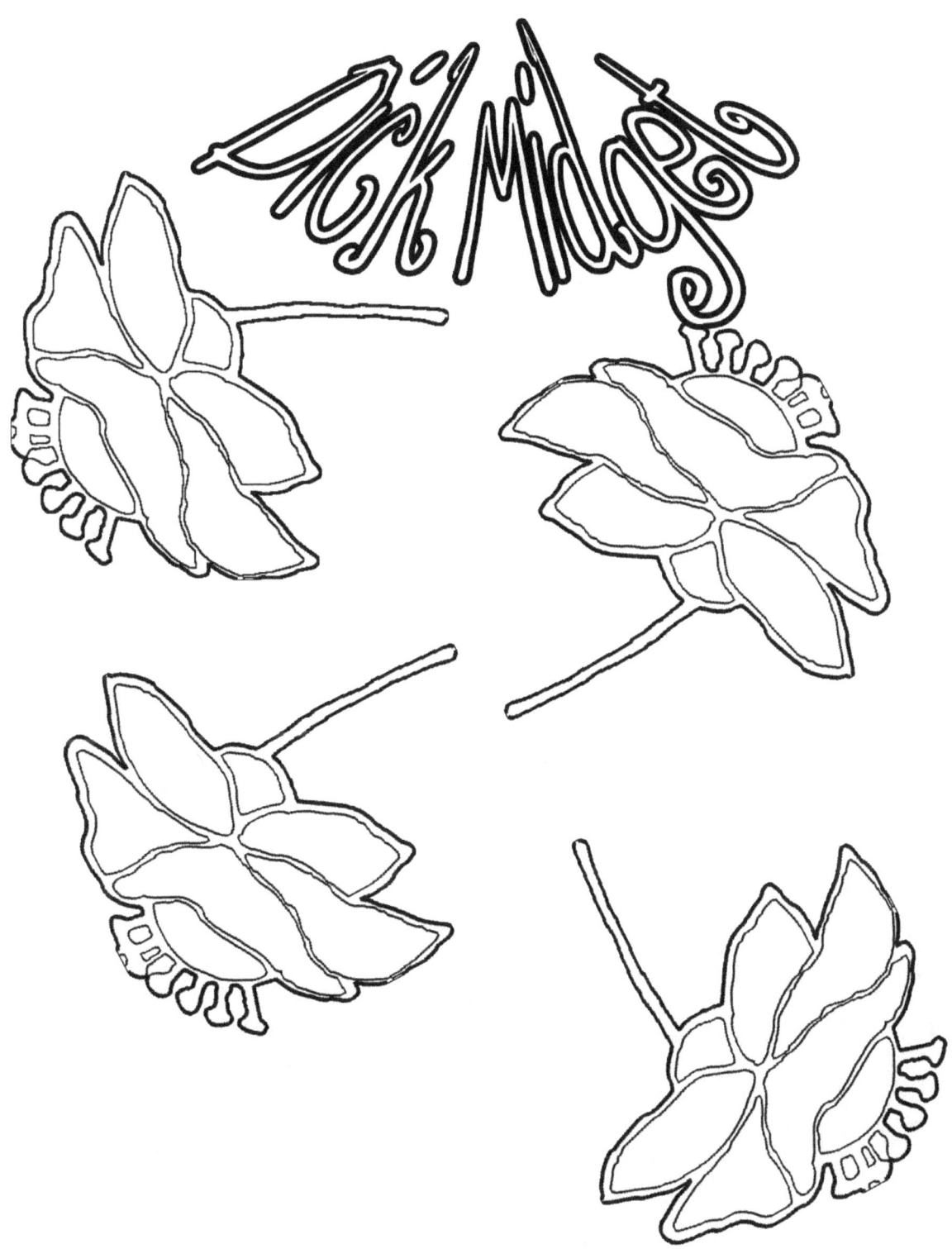

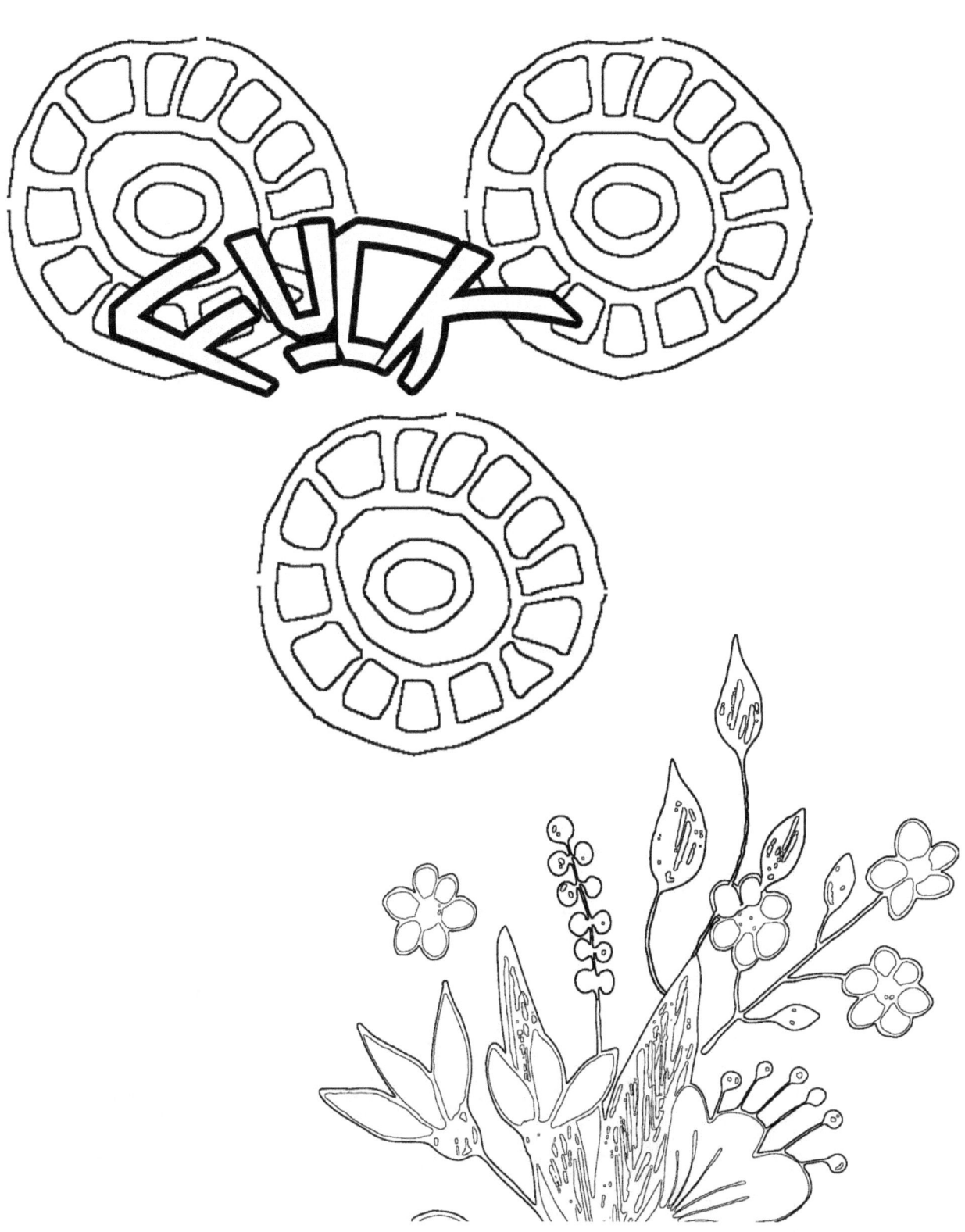

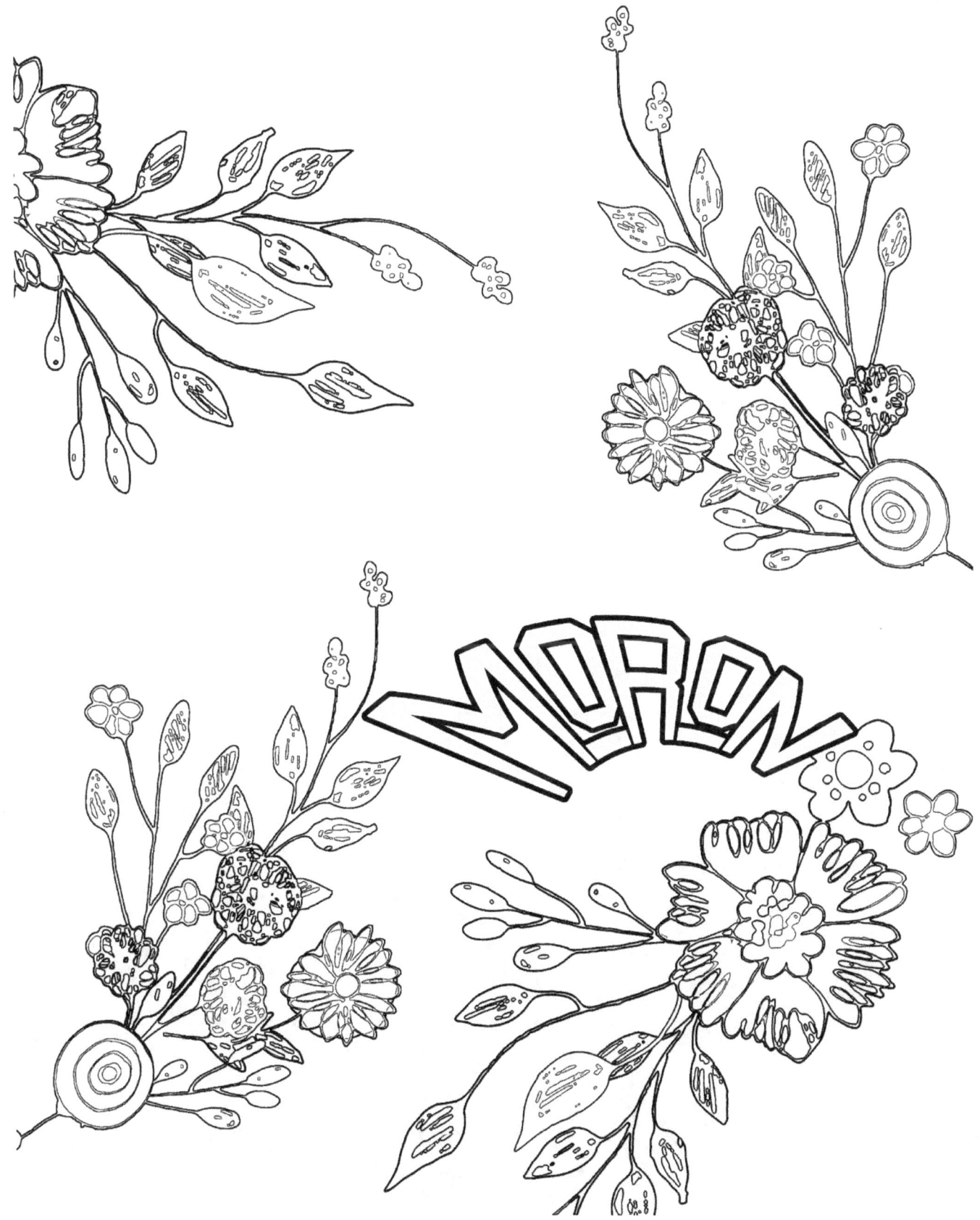

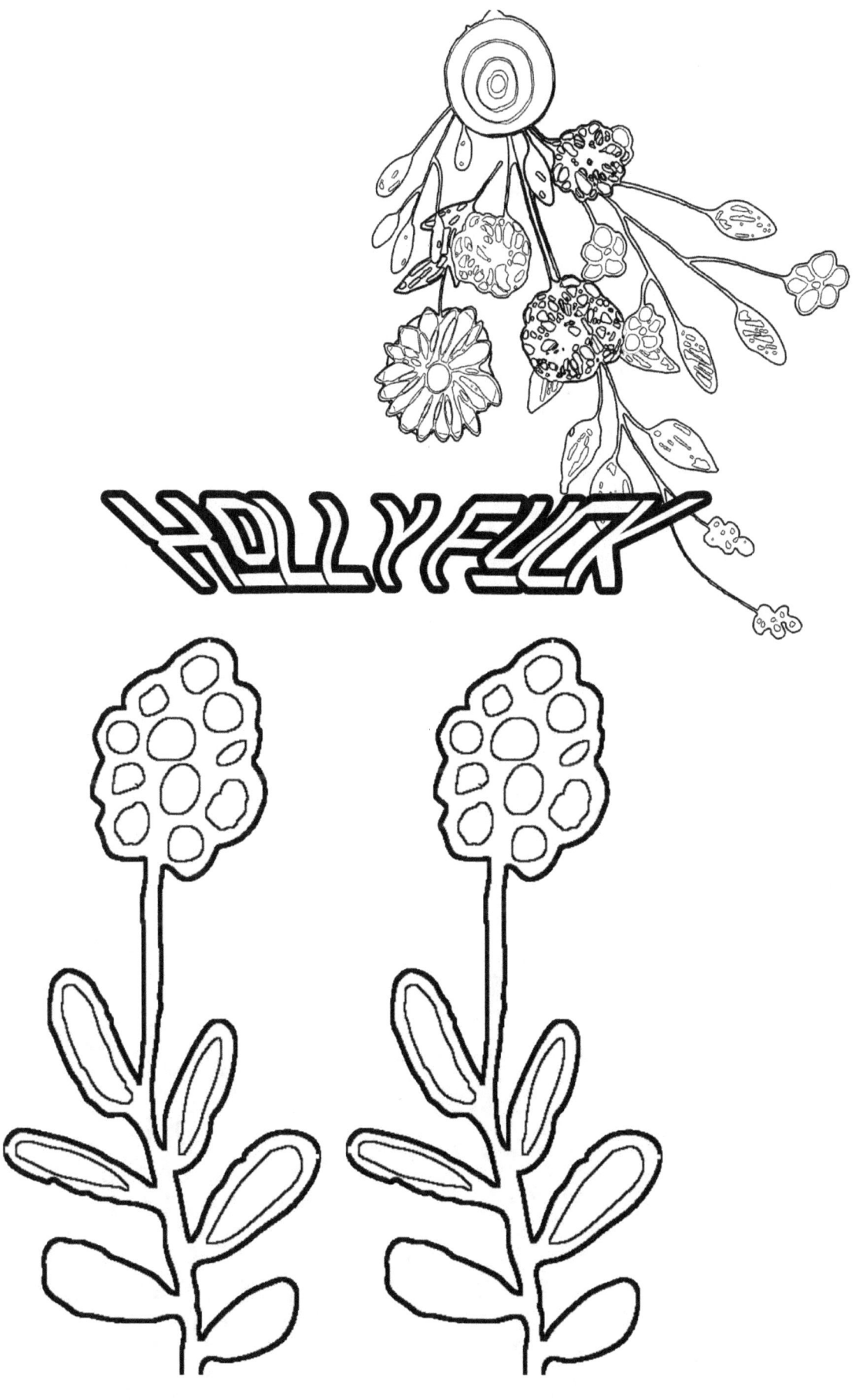

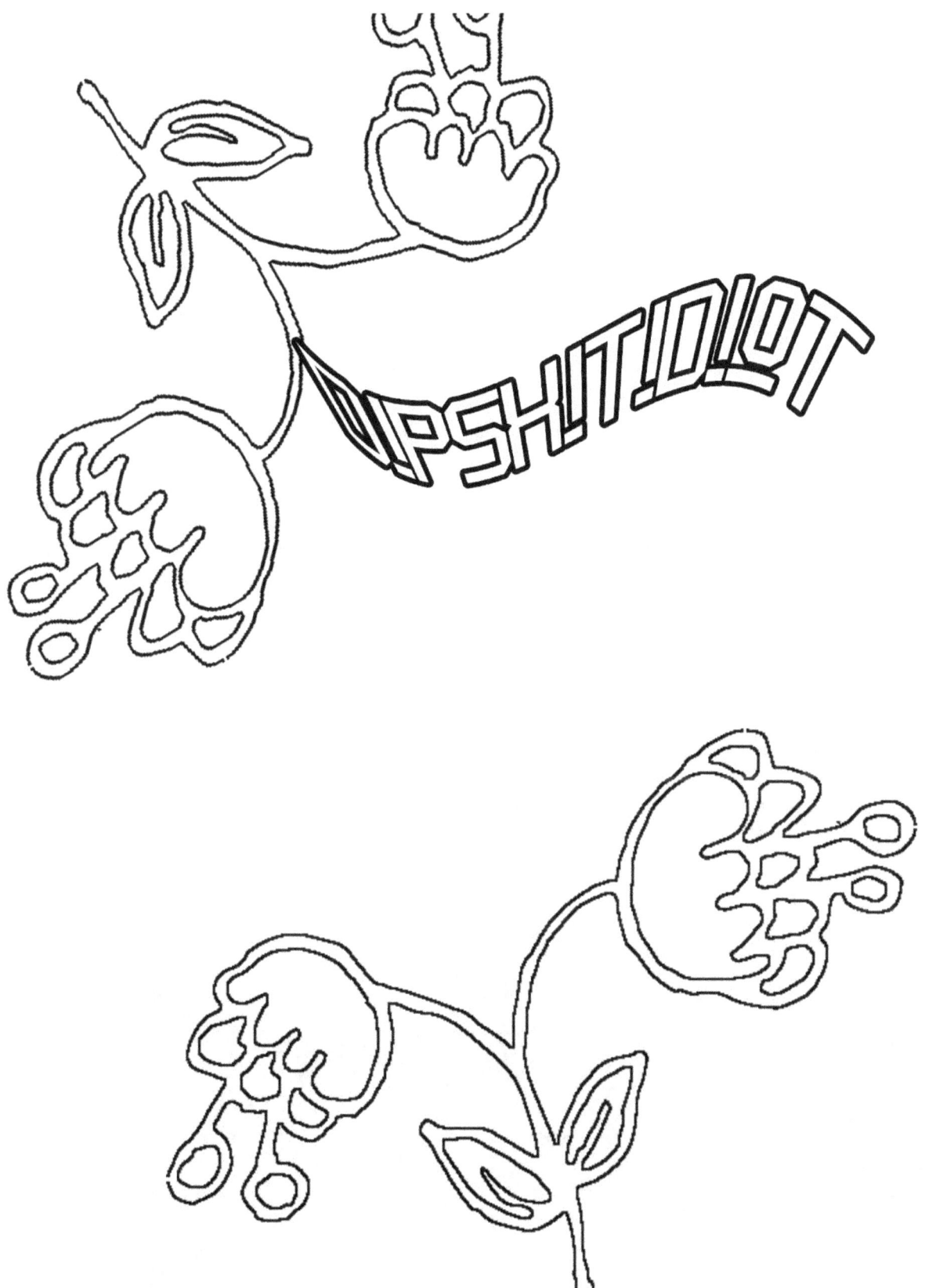

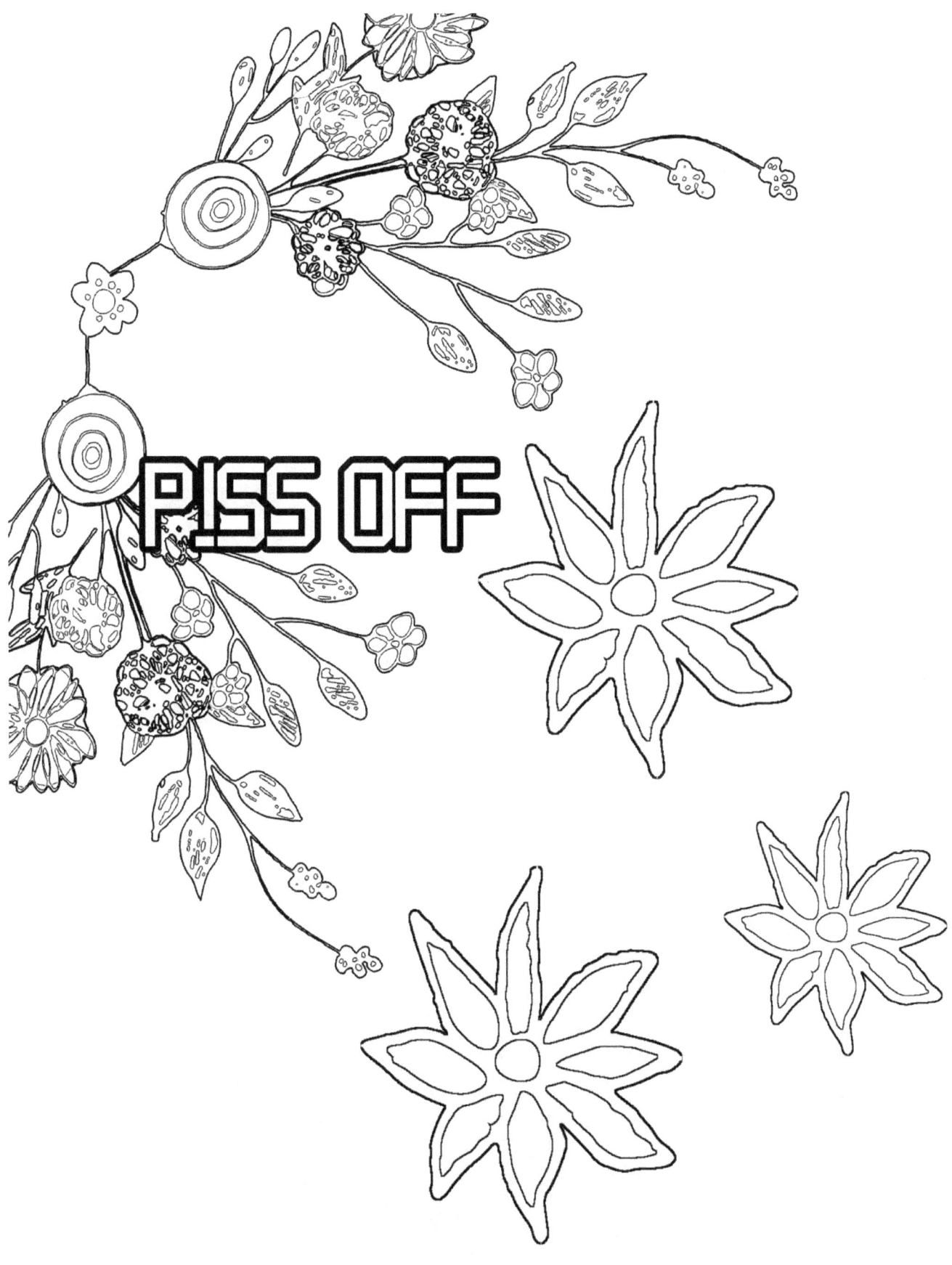

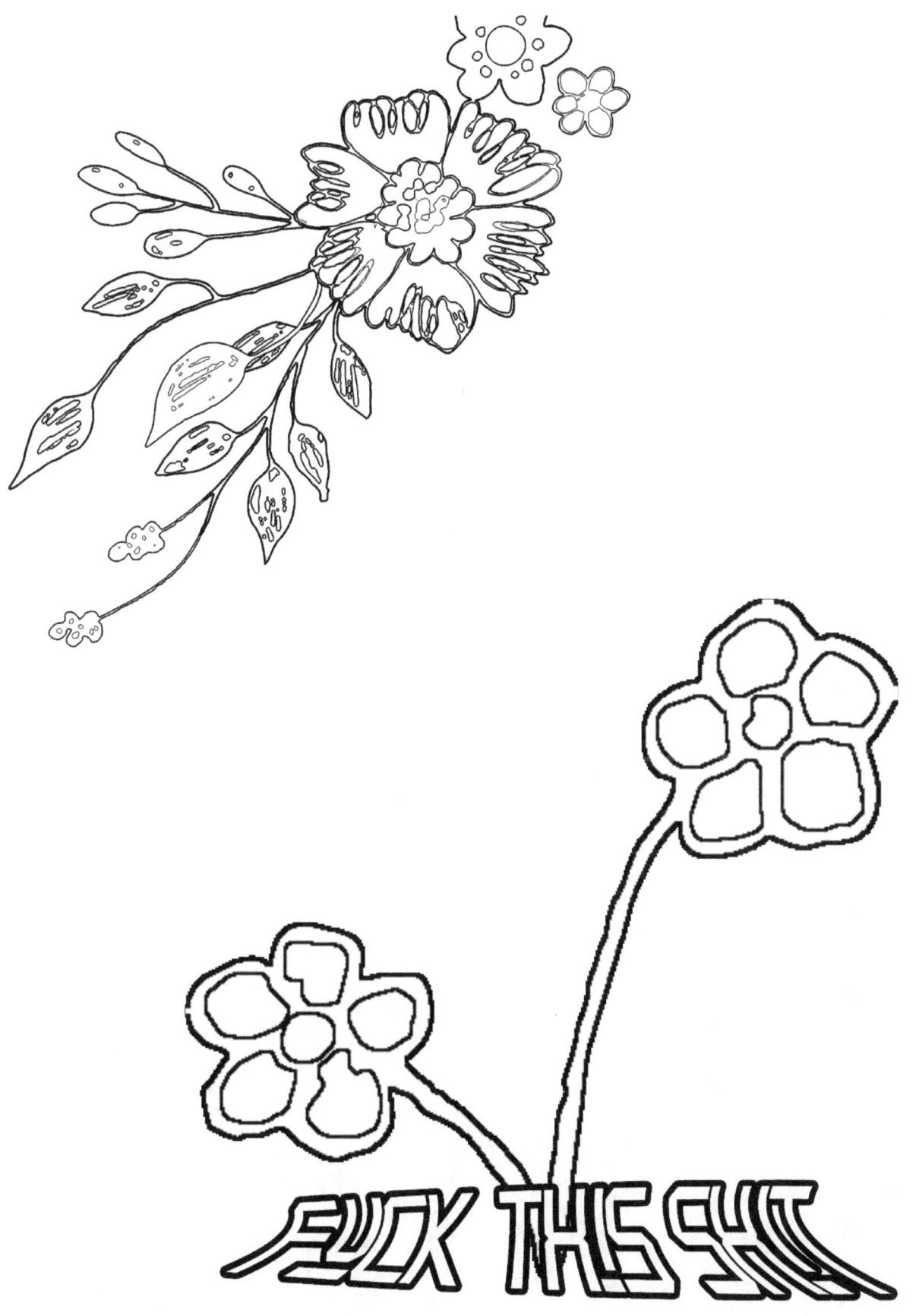

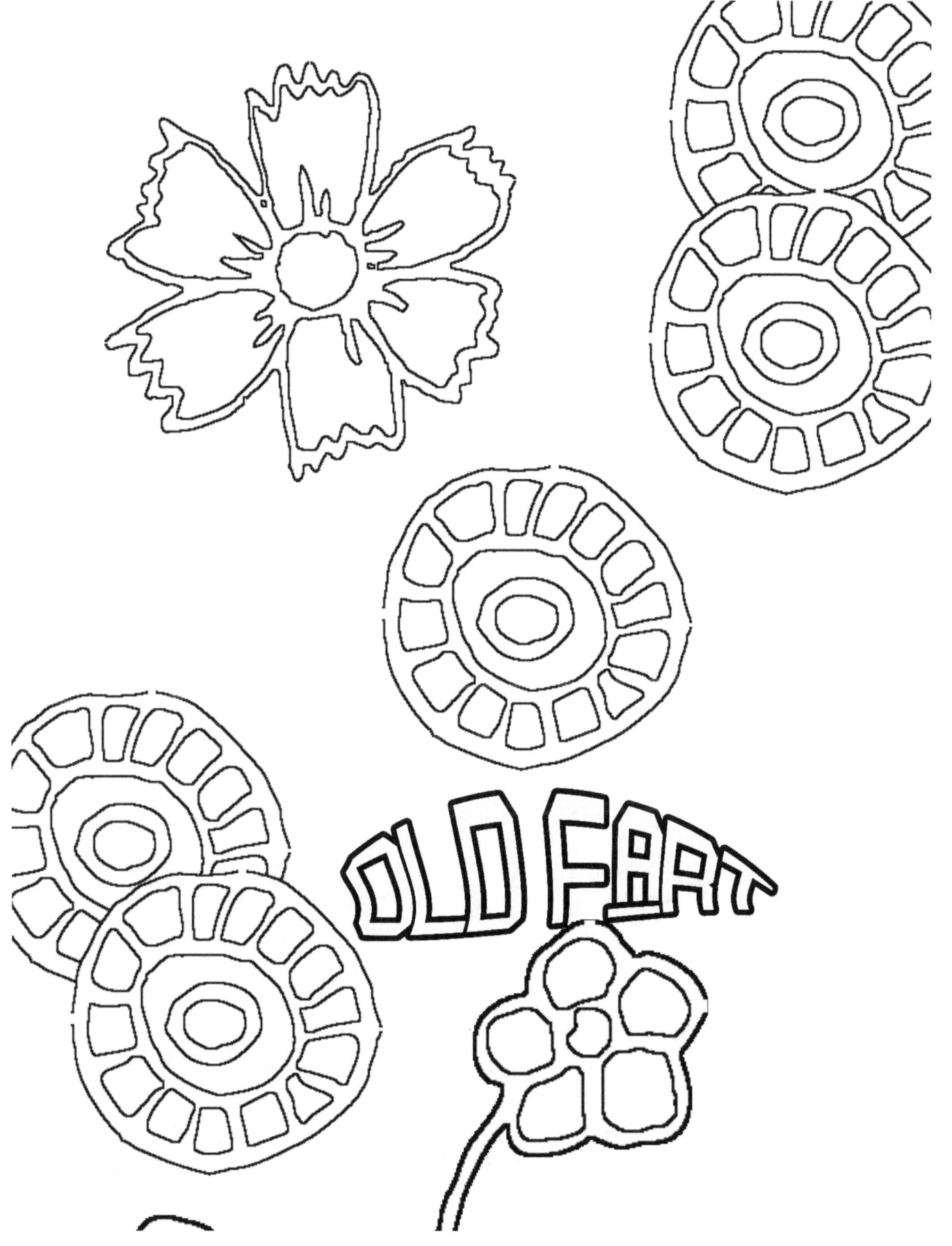

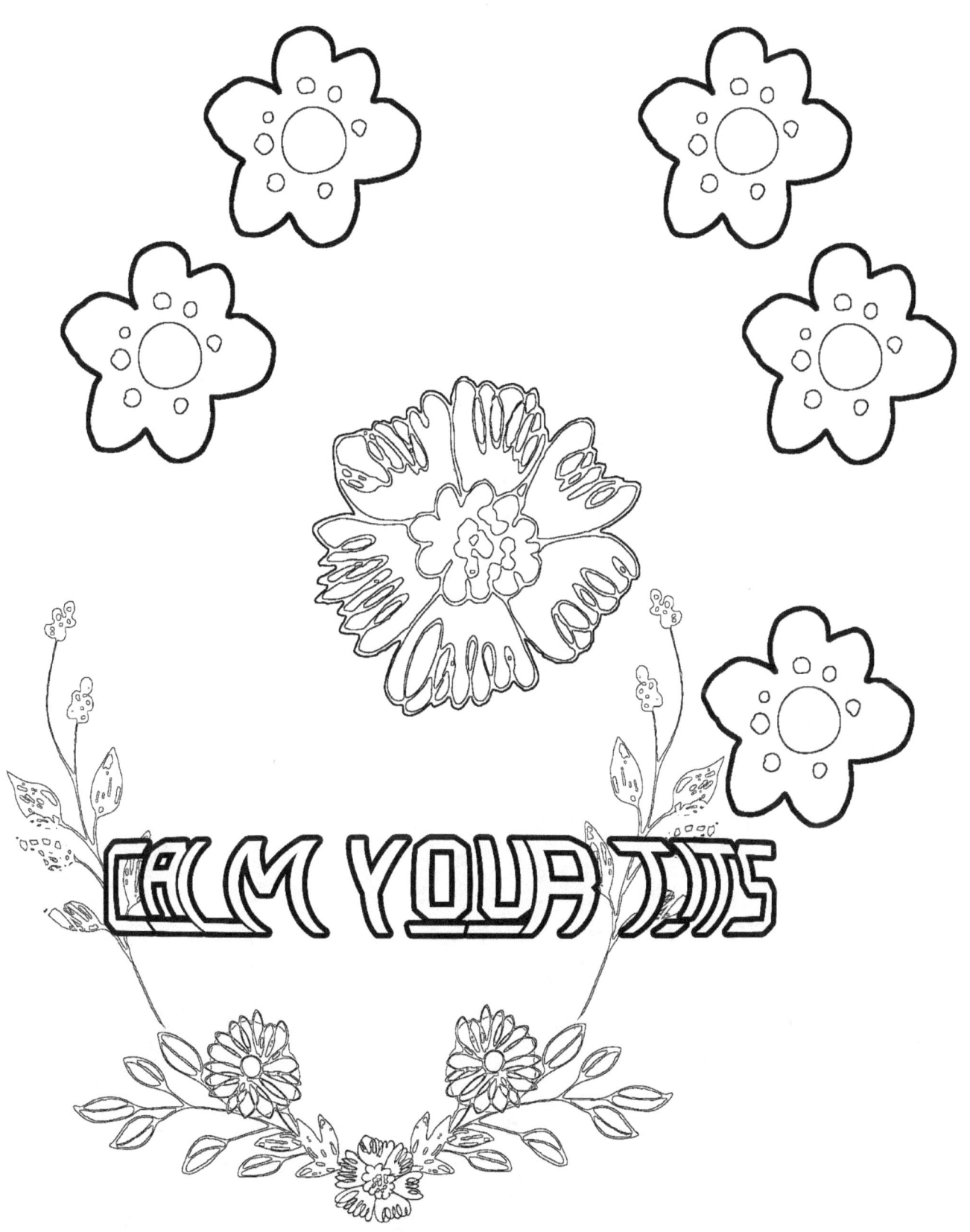

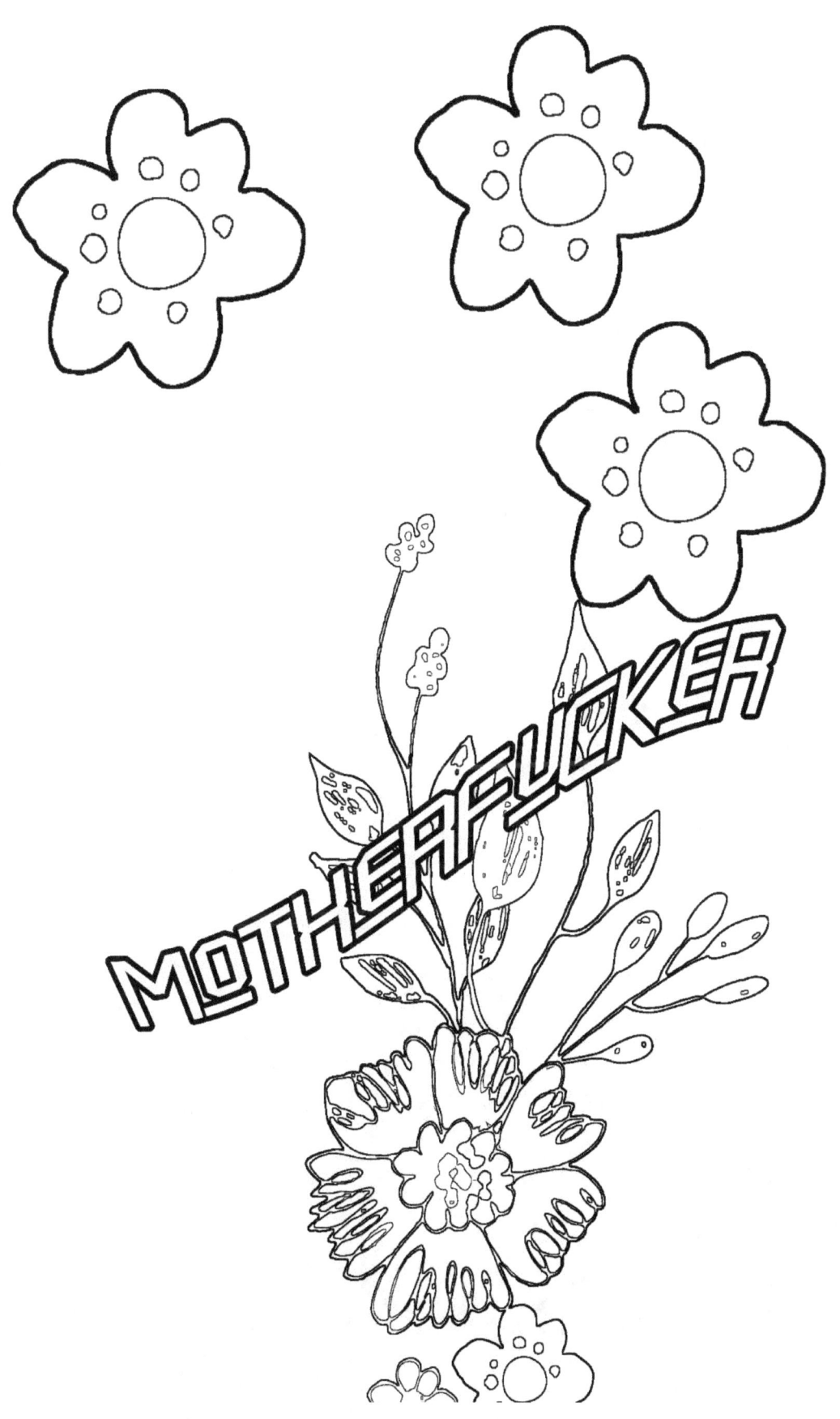

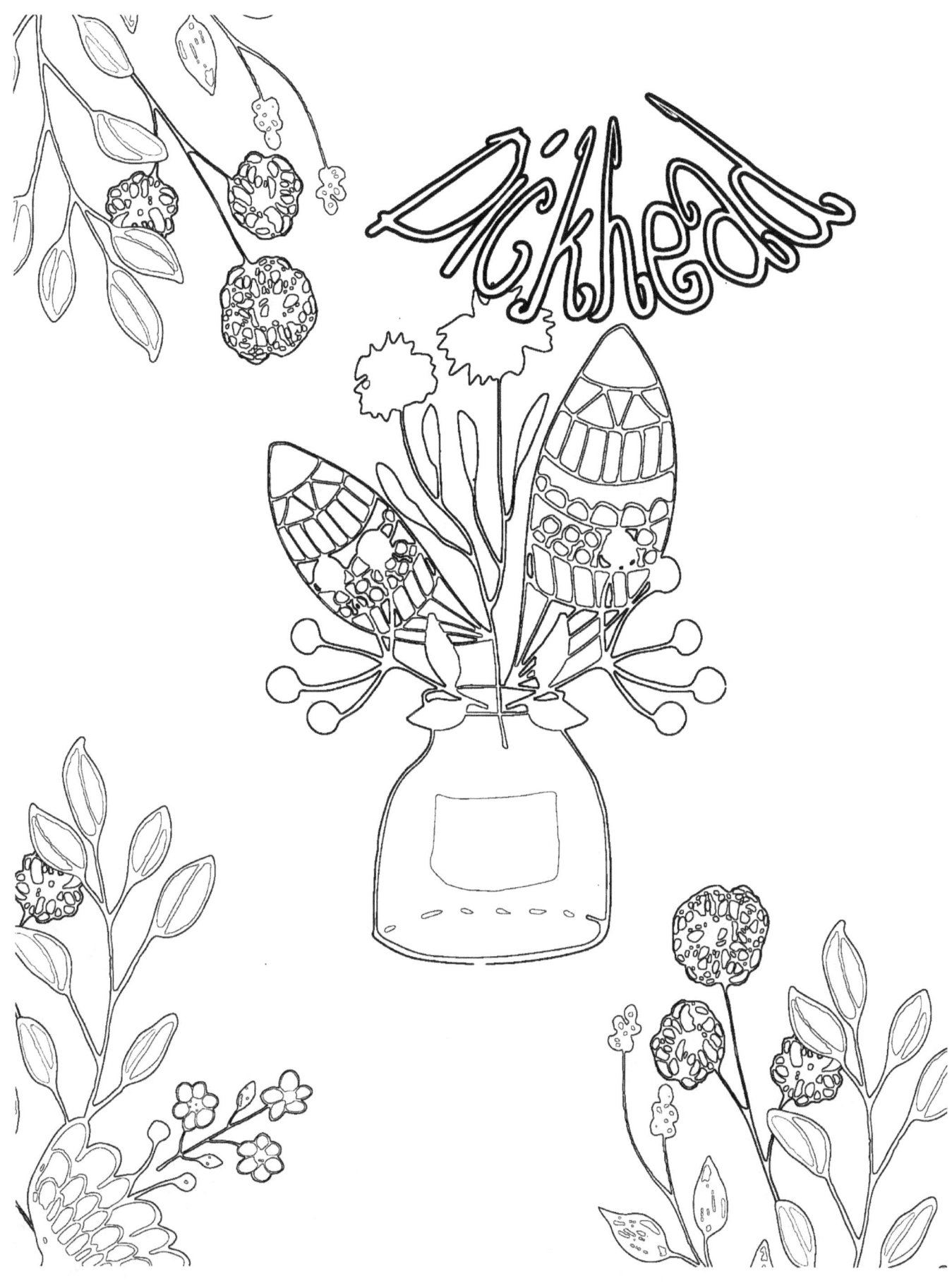

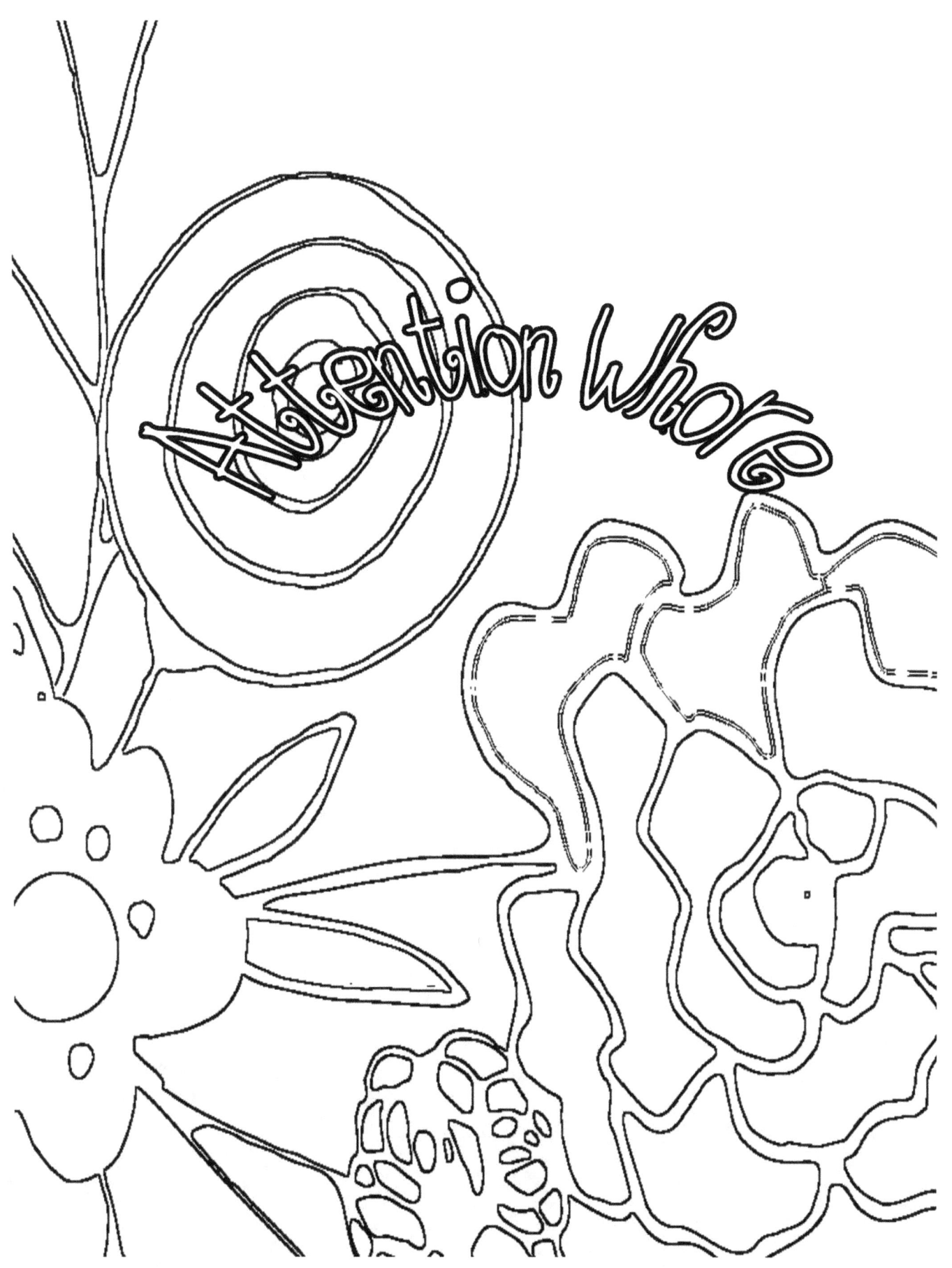

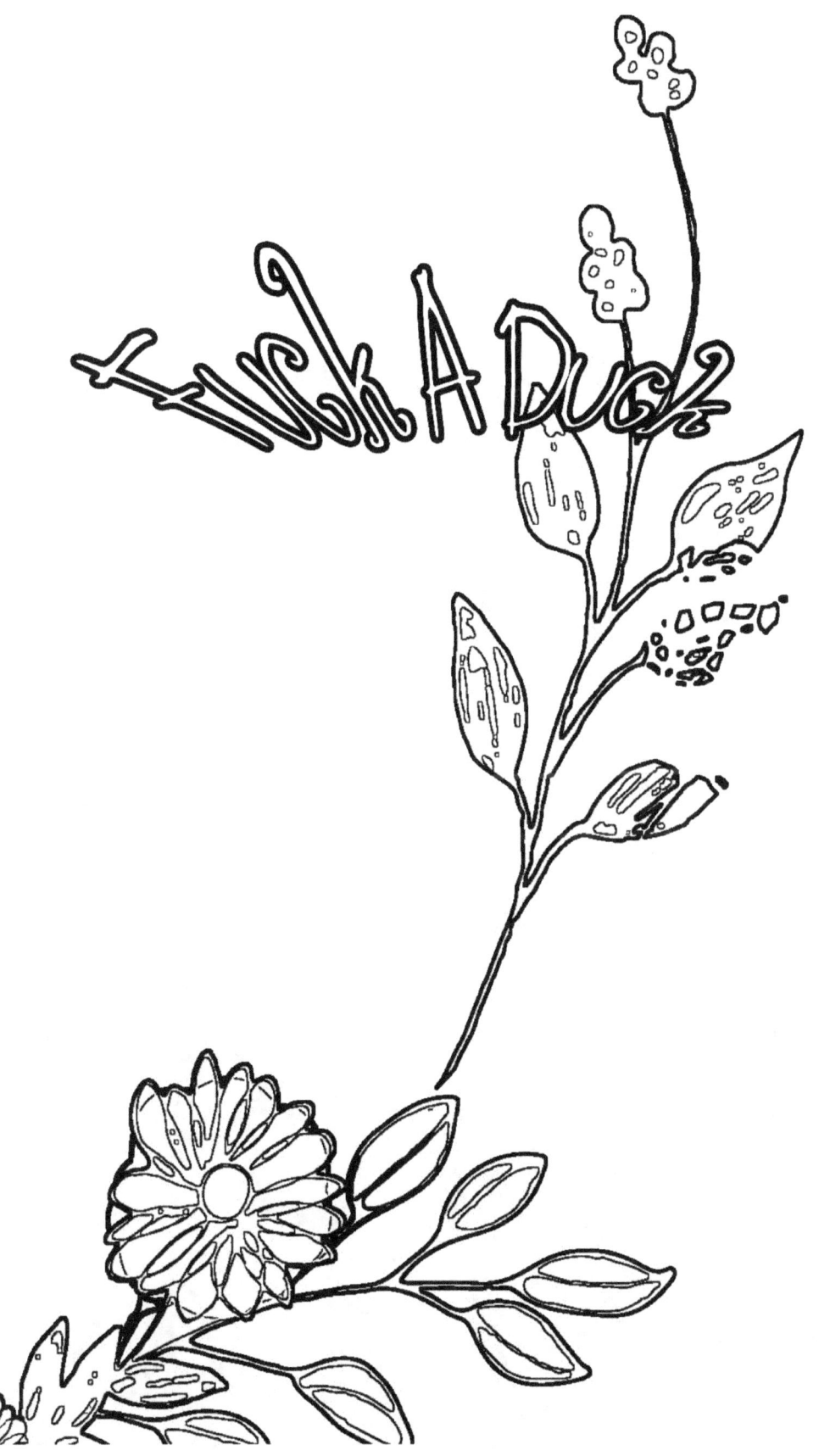

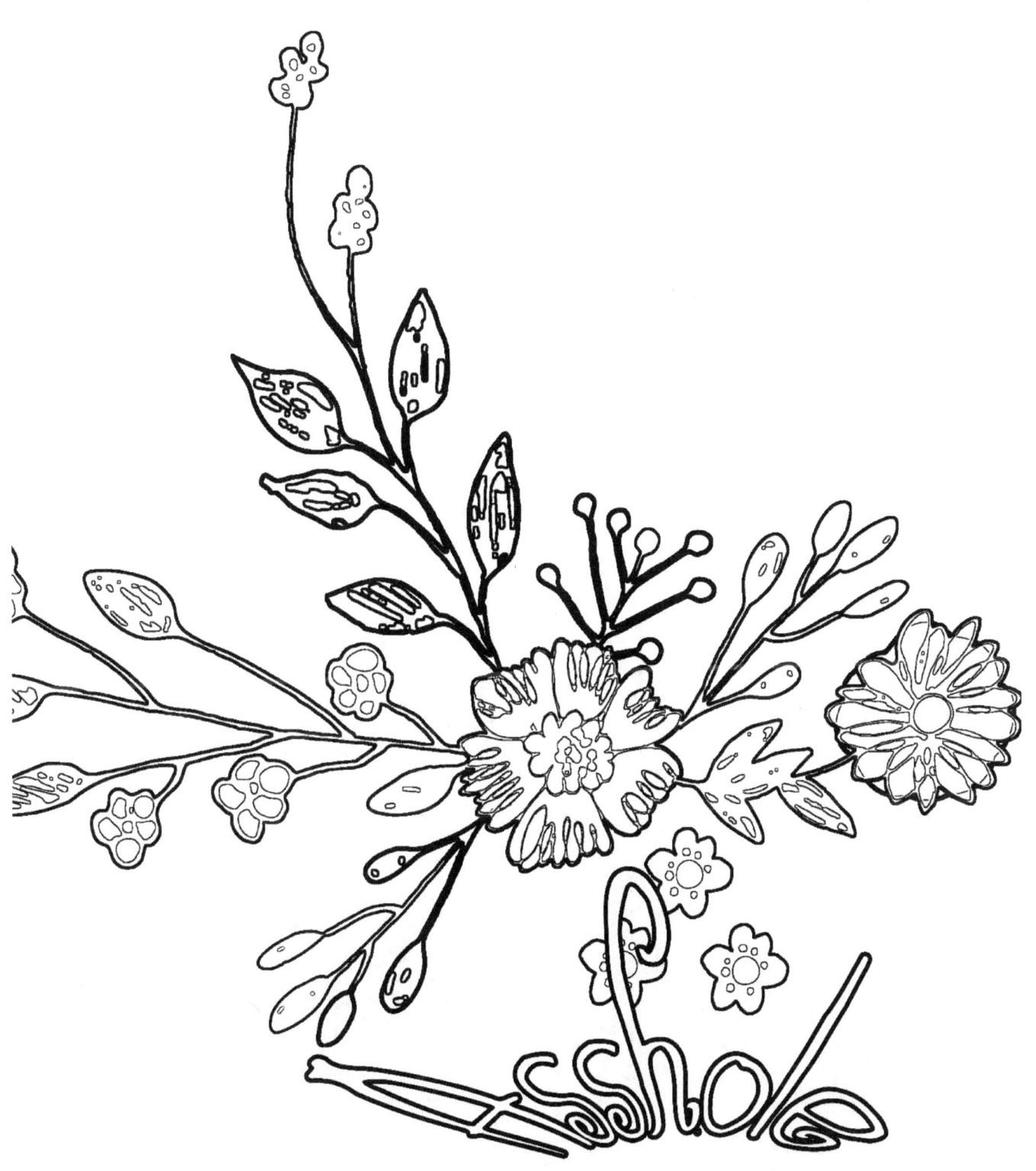

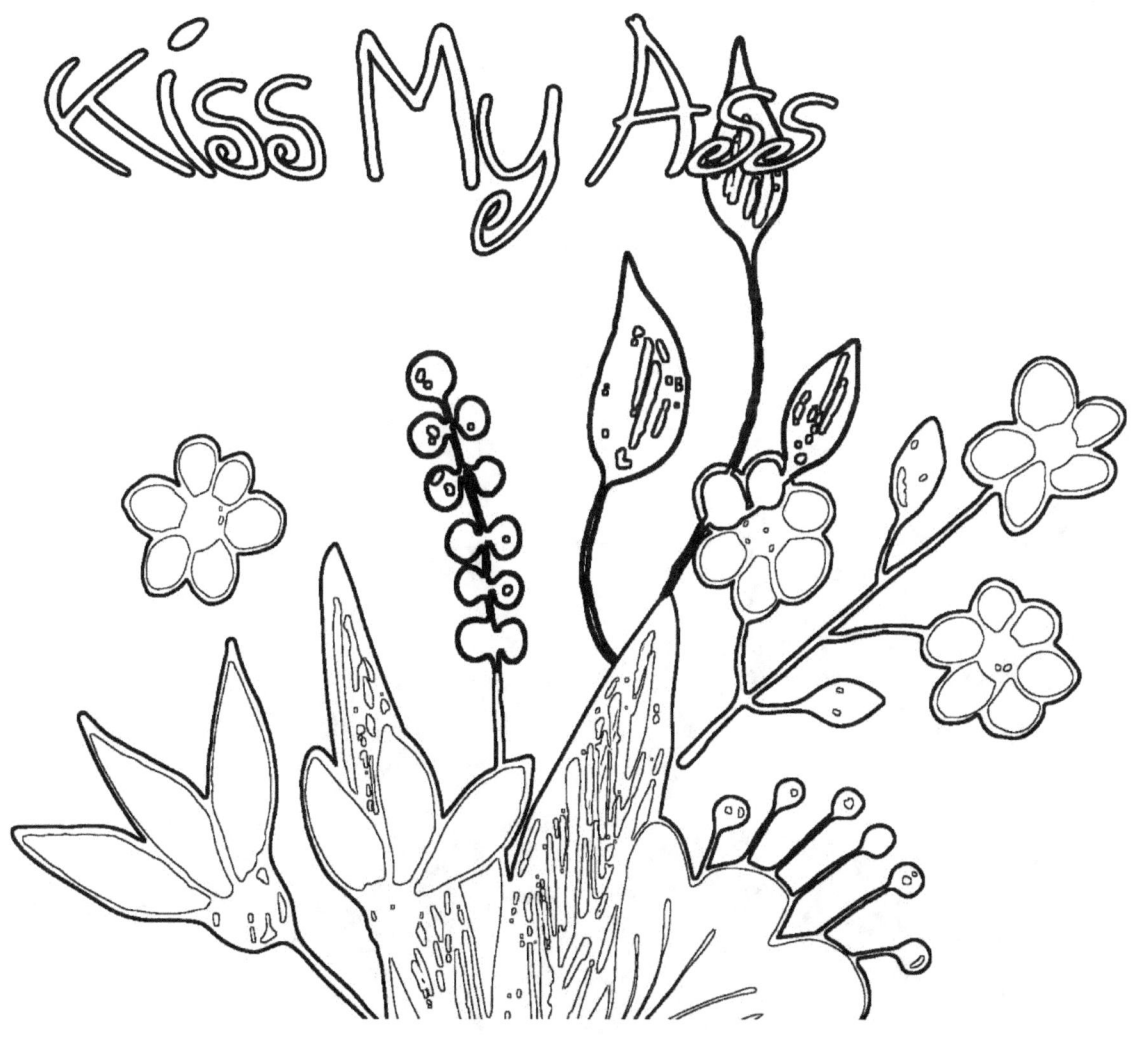

cunt Fall

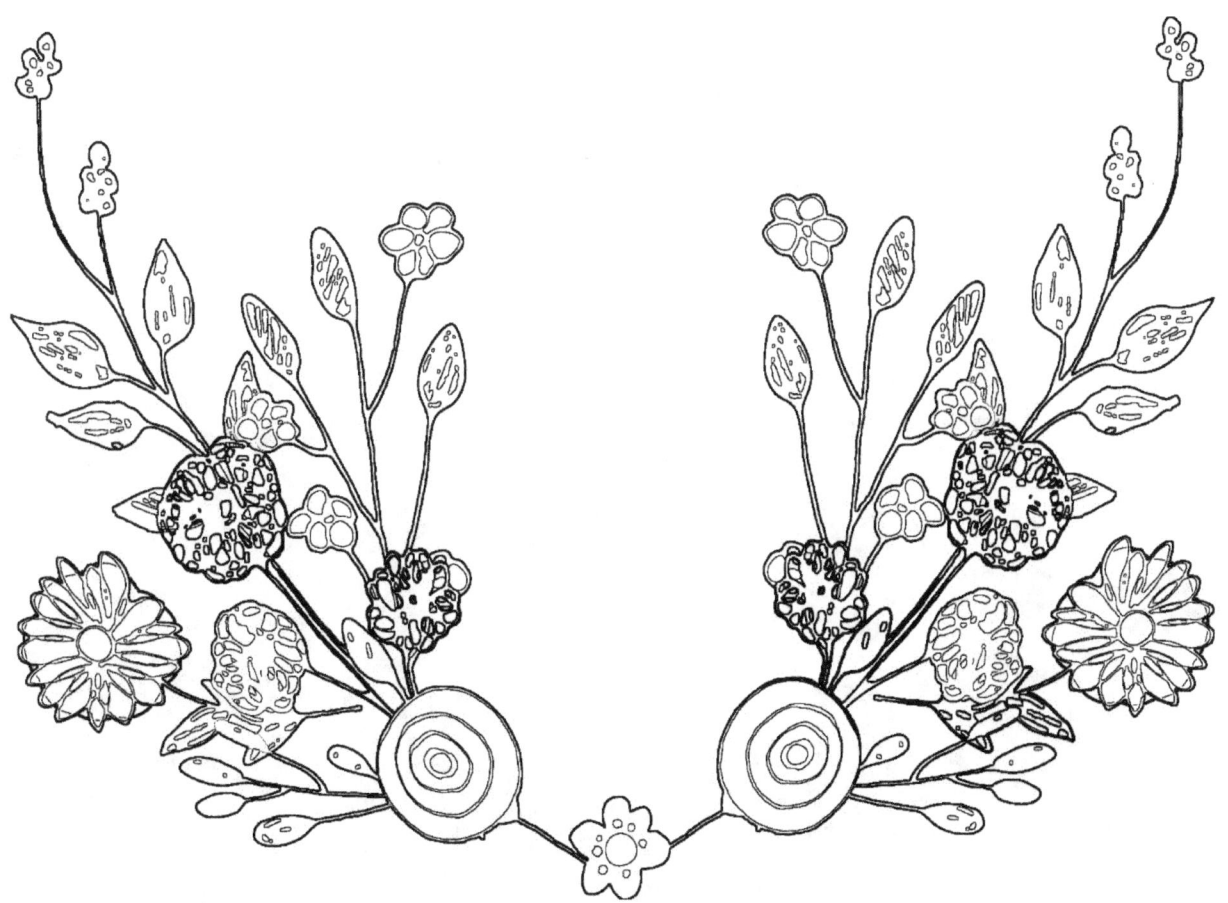

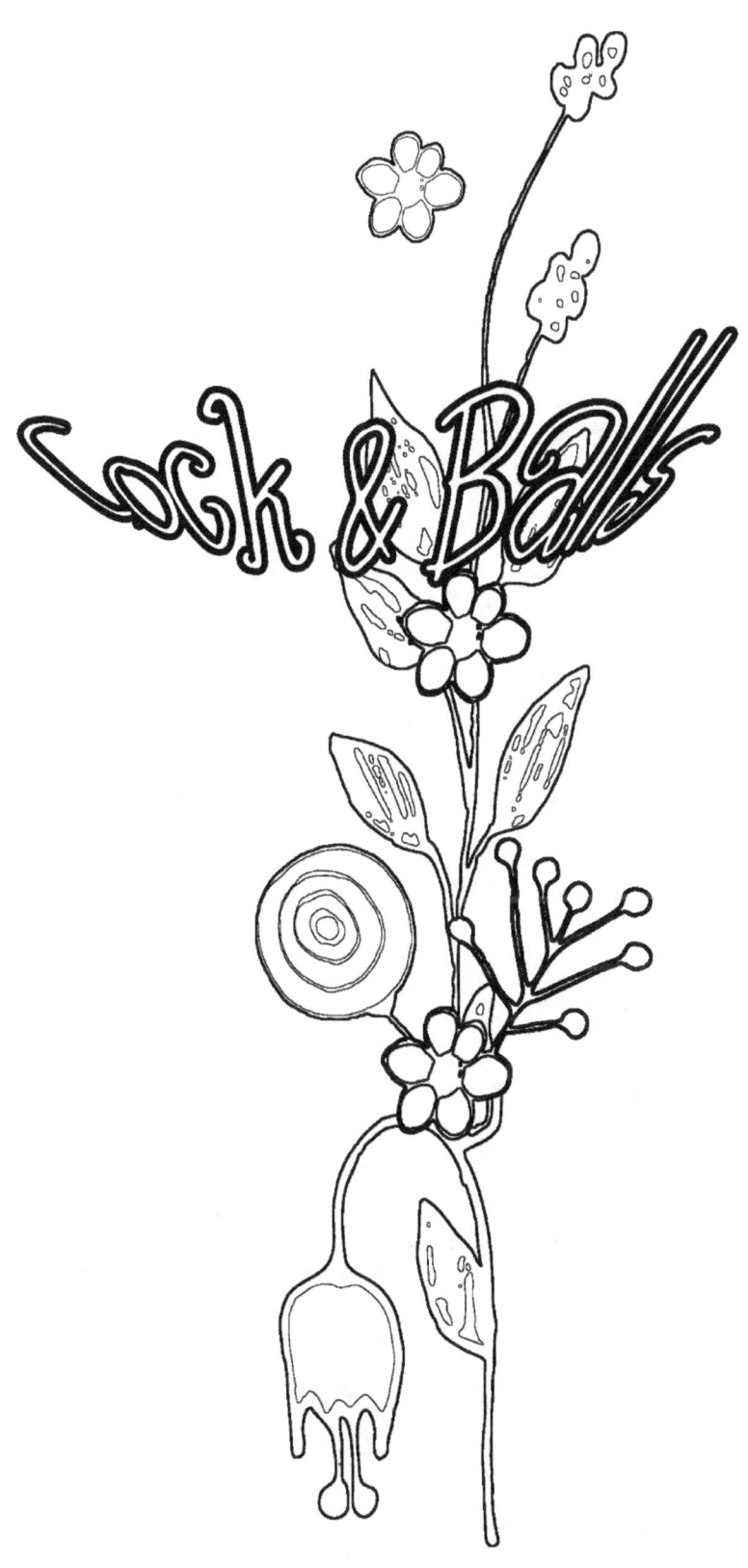

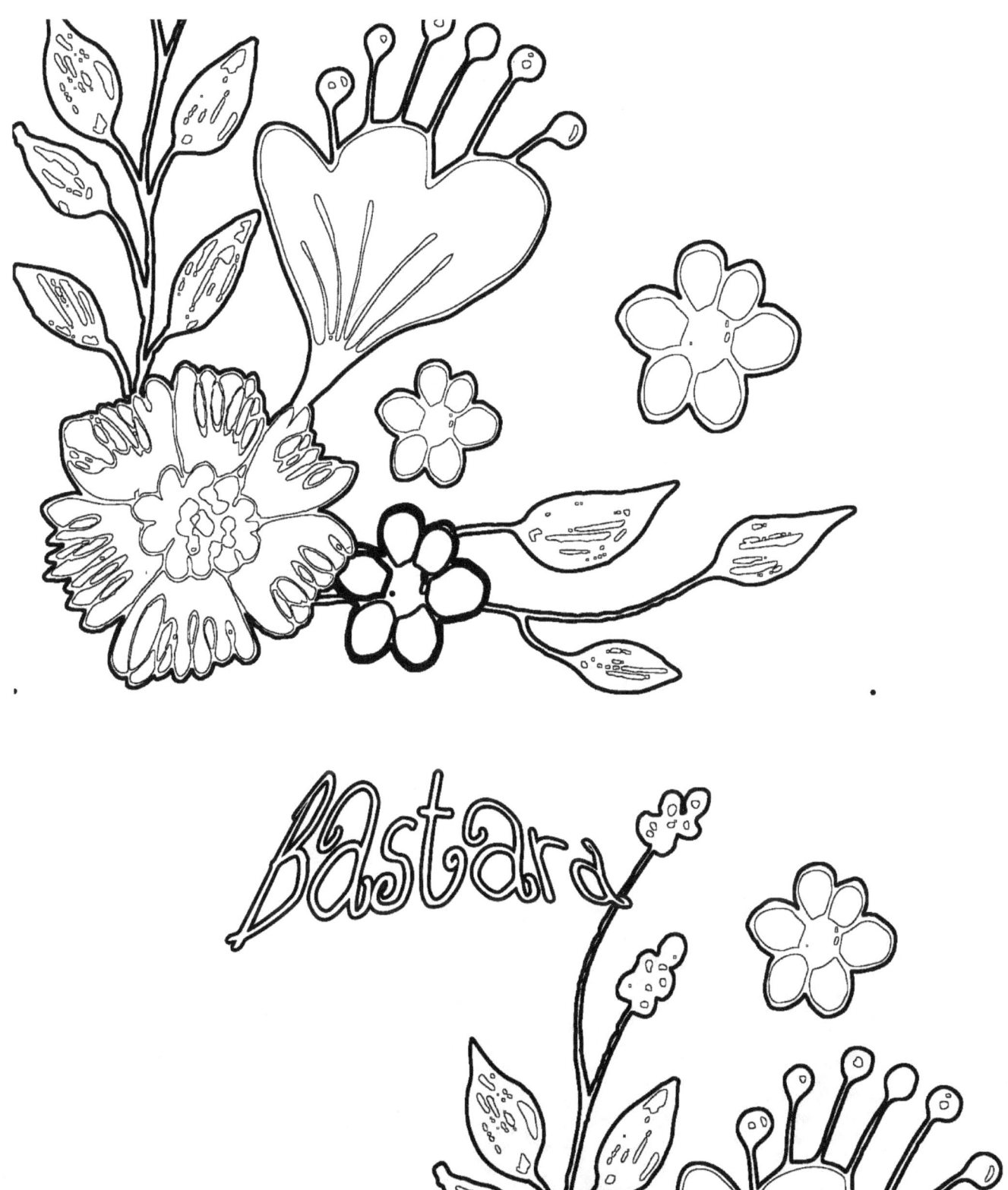

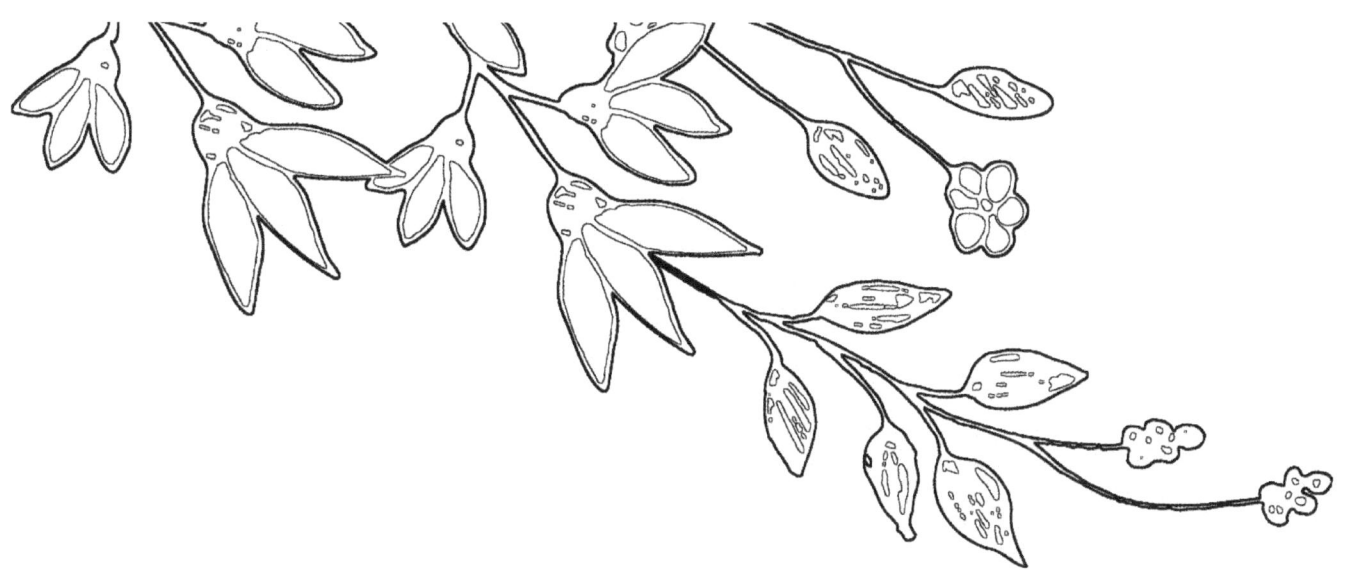

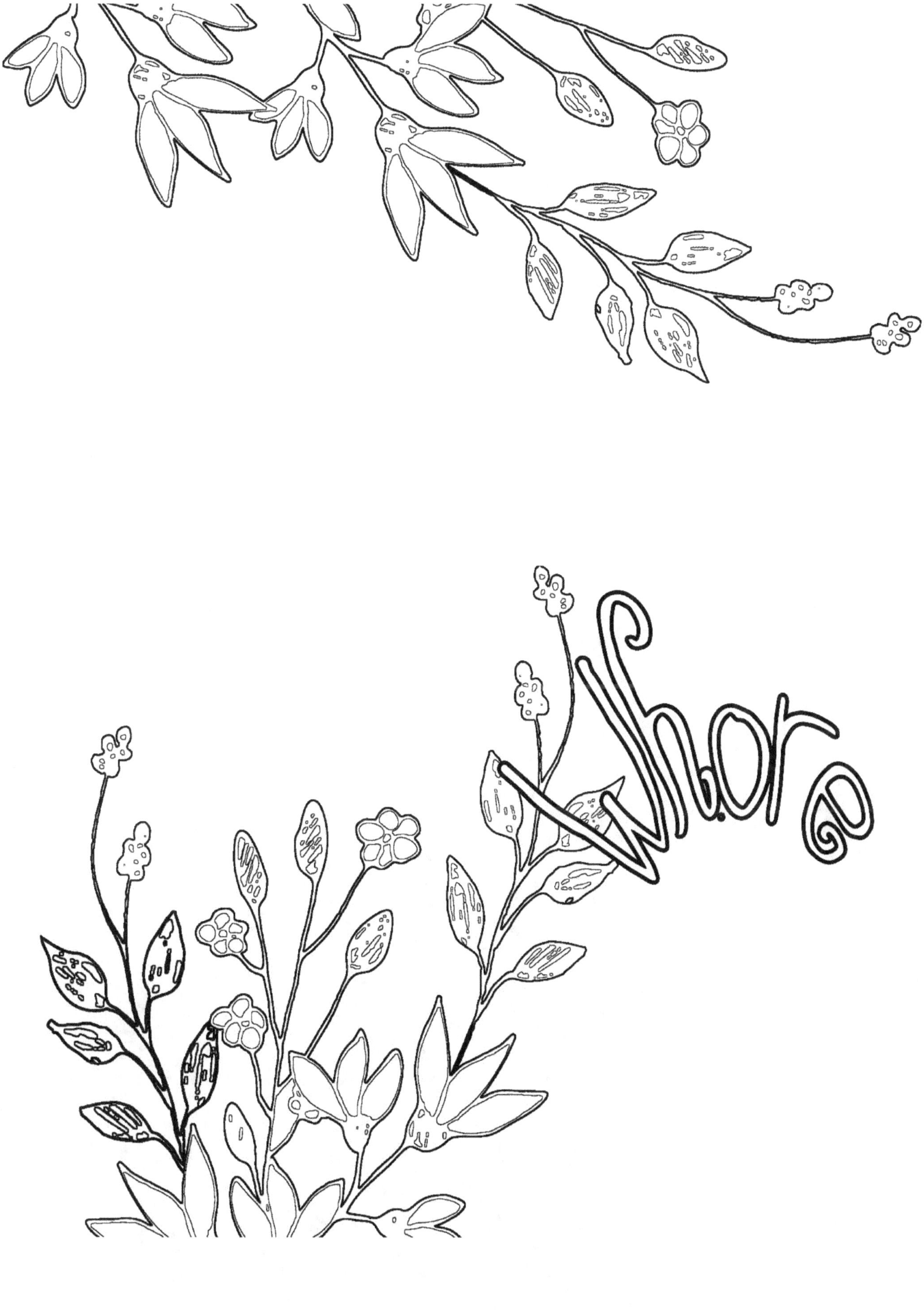

Whore

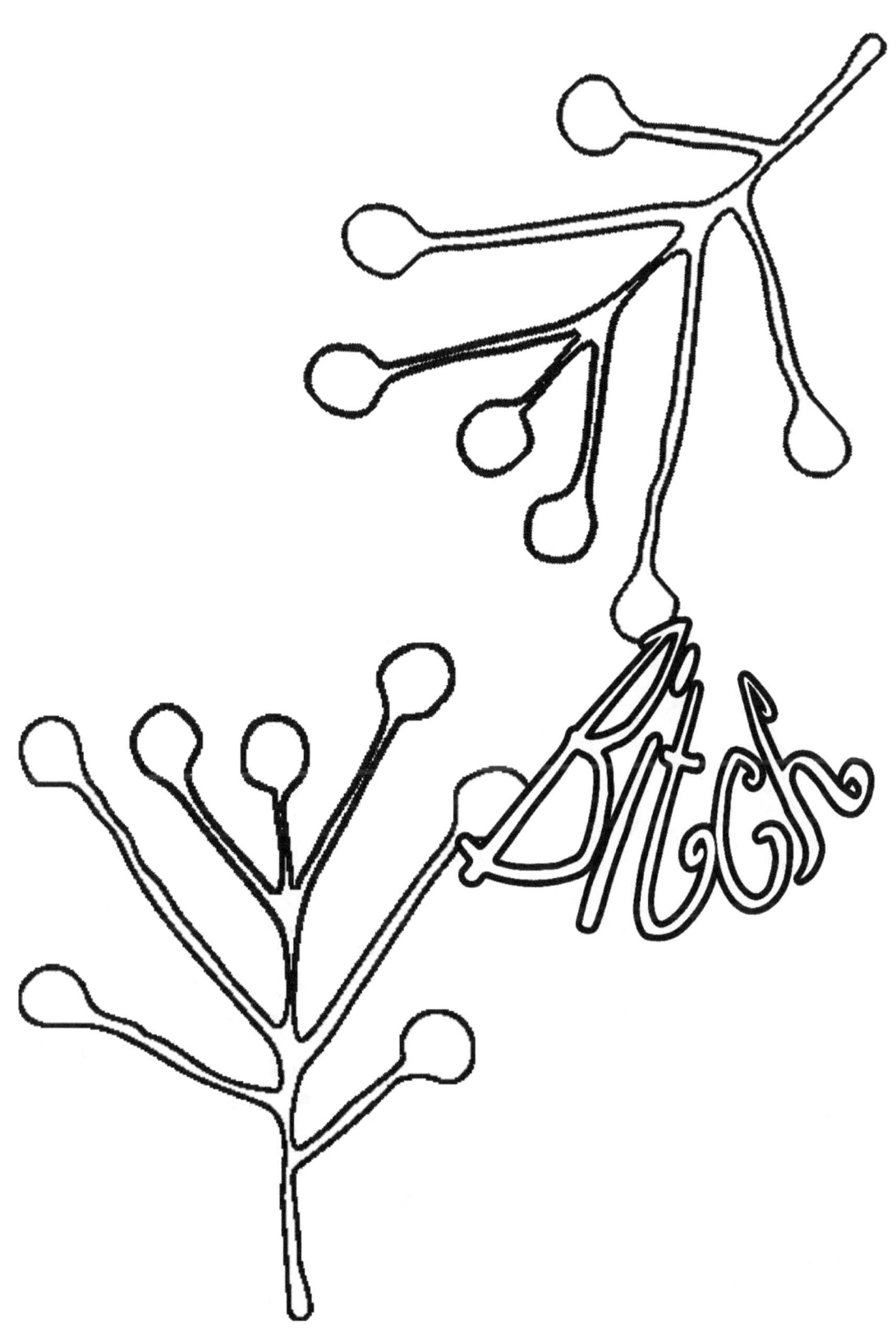

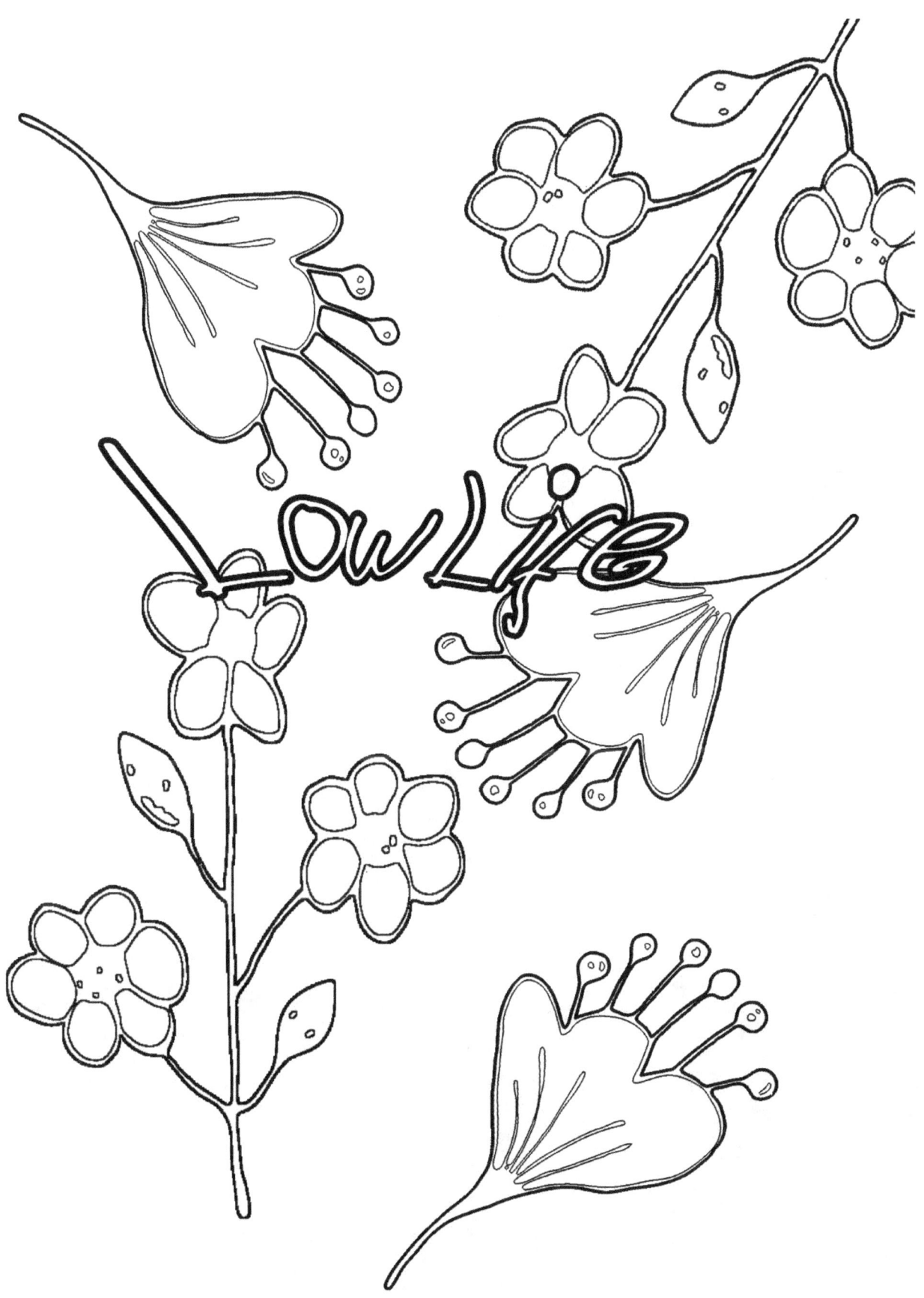

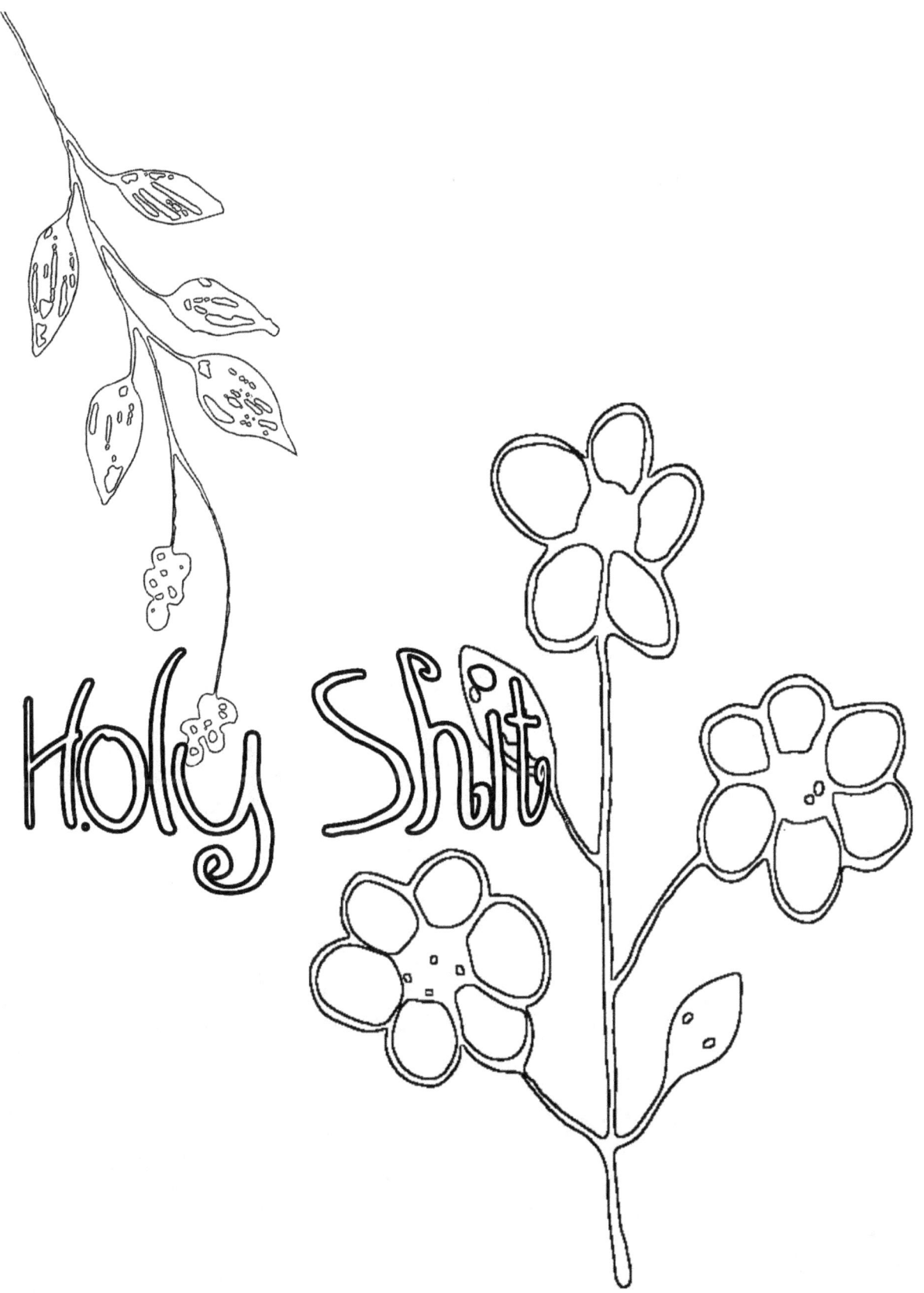

www.ingramcontent.com/pod-product-compliance
Lightning Source LLC
Chambersburg PA
CBHW081749170526
45167CB00009B/3978